This Boys Rock Career Coloring Book Belongs To

_____

Future Global Leader!

A is for

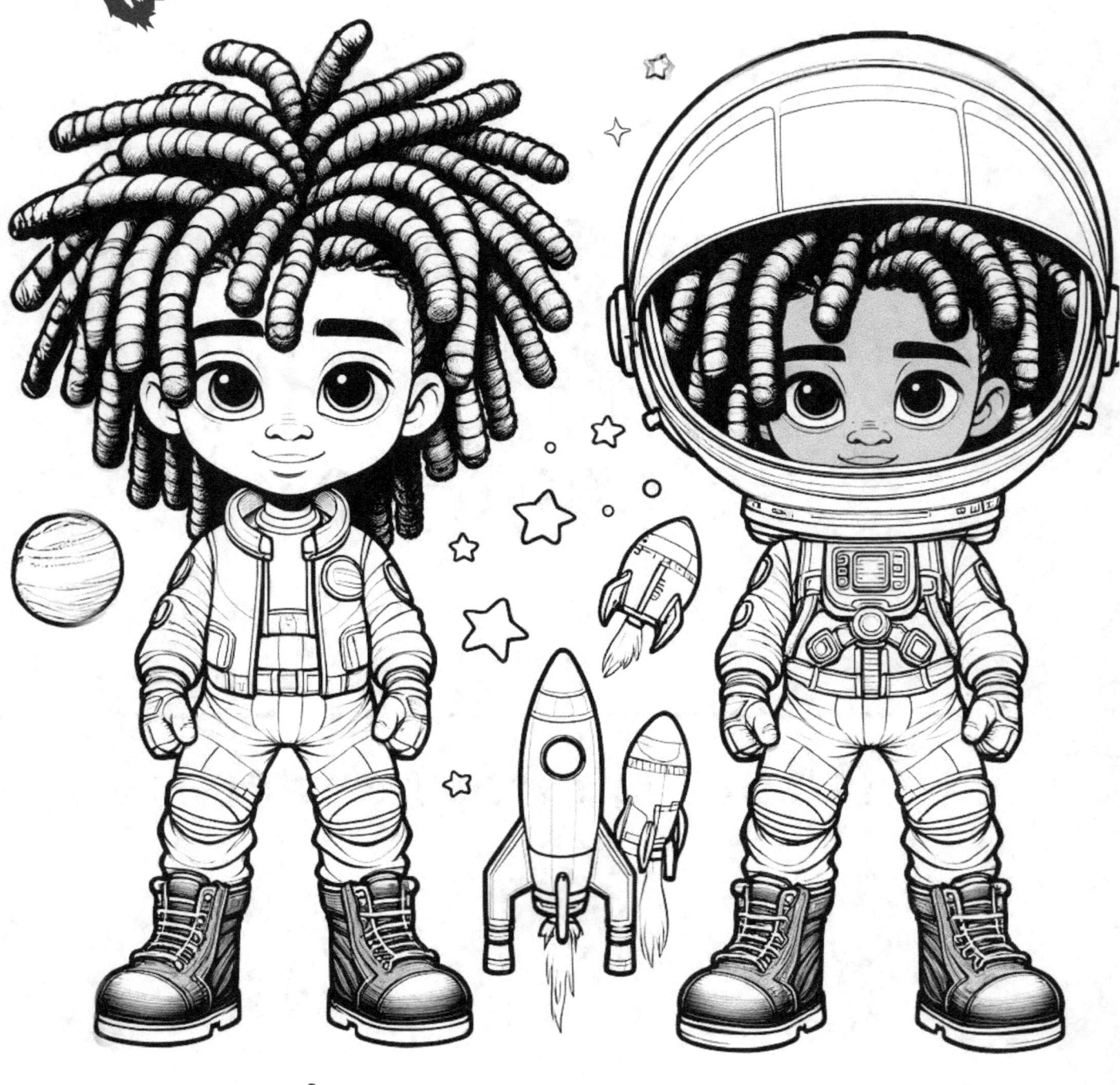

ASTRONAUT

B is for

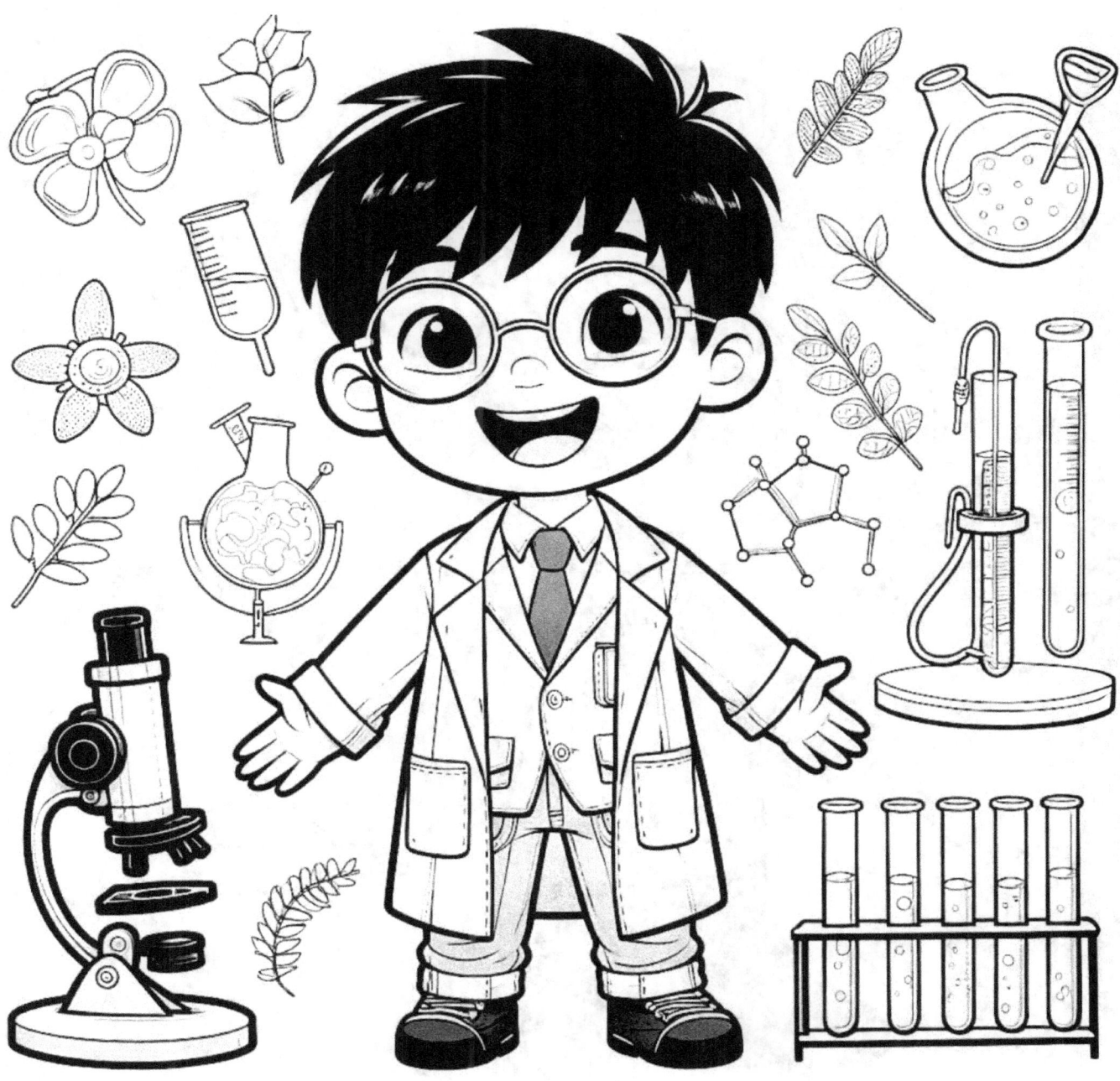

BIOLOGIST

C Is for

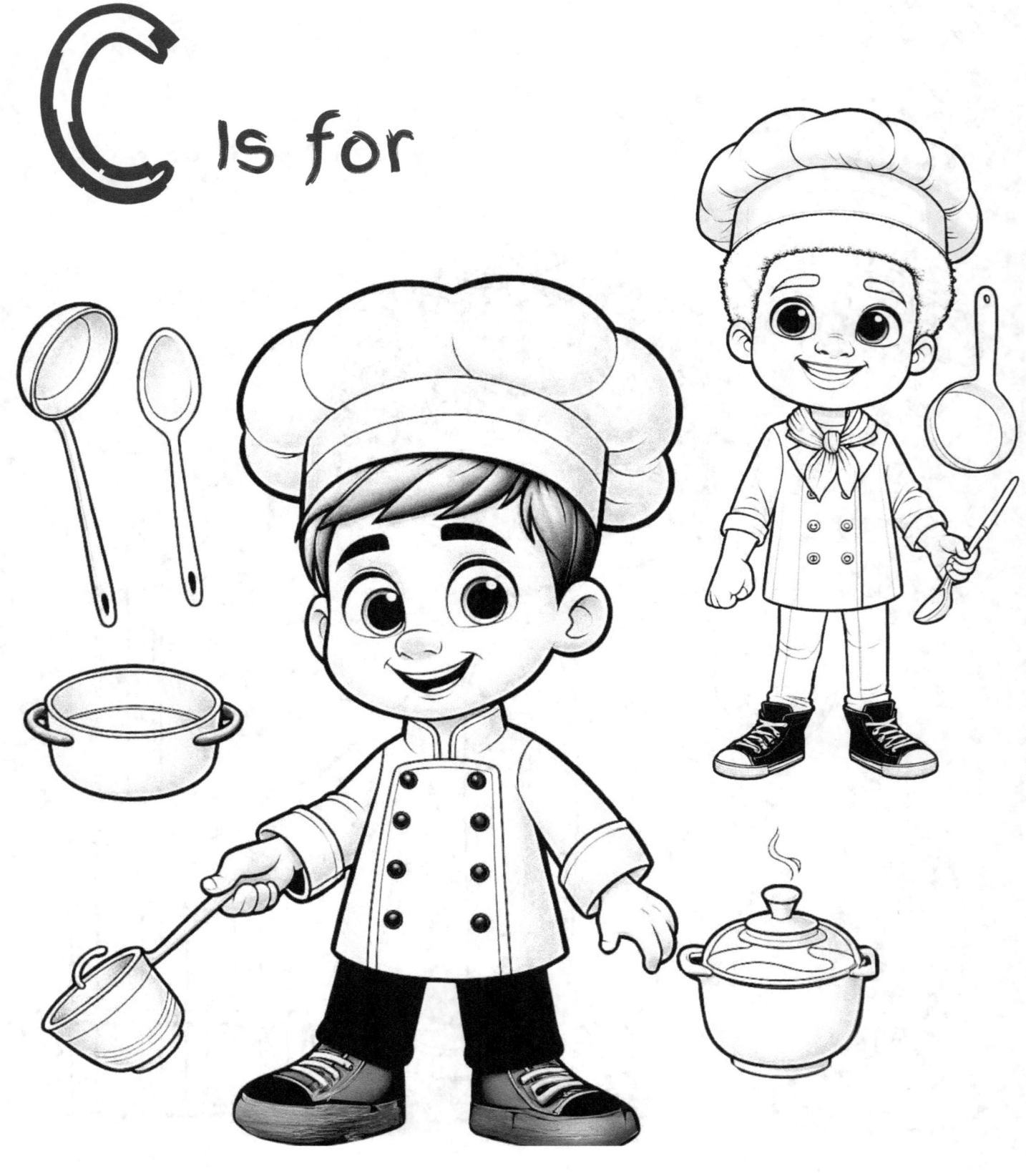

CHEF

D is for

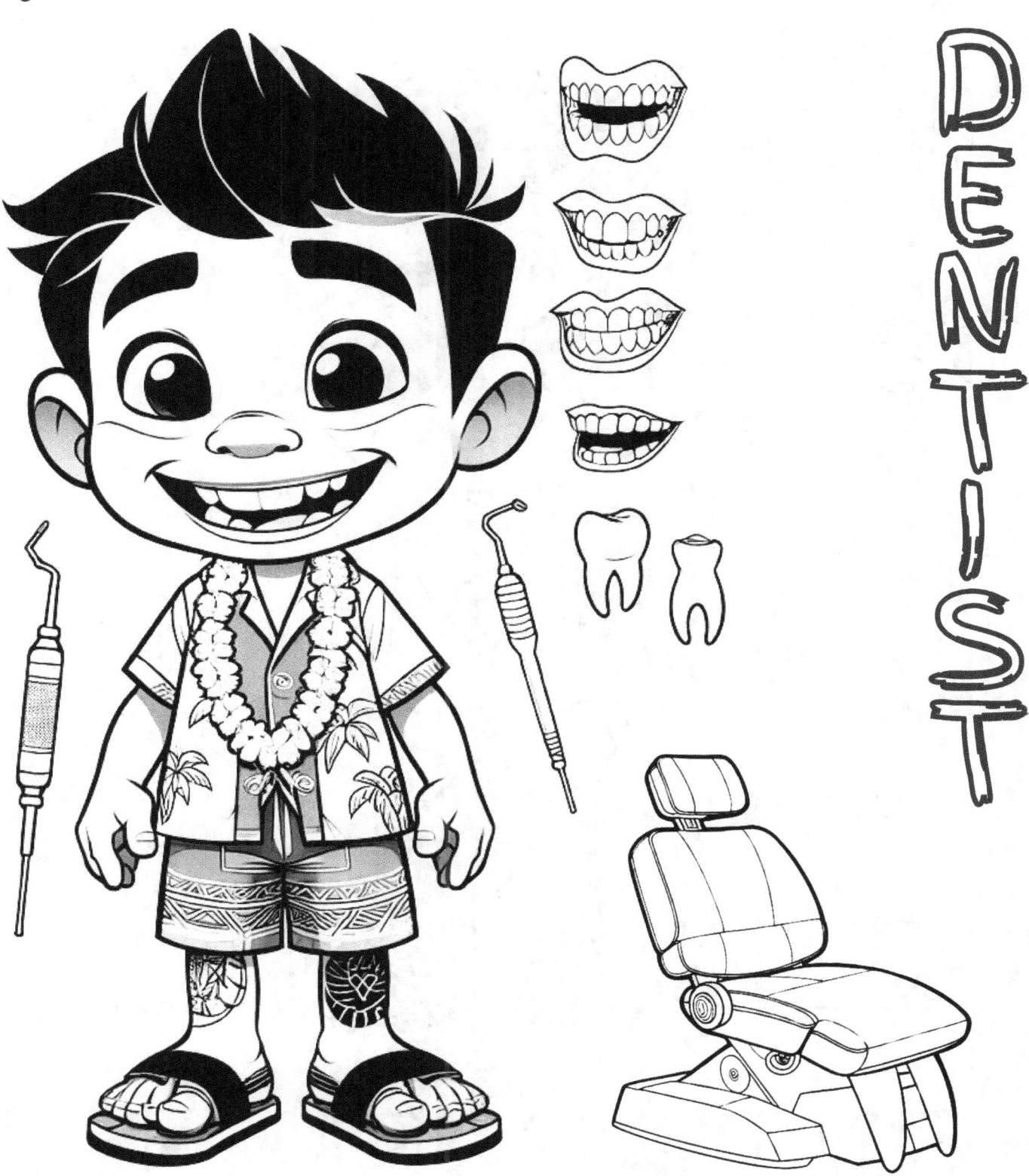

DENTIST

E Is for

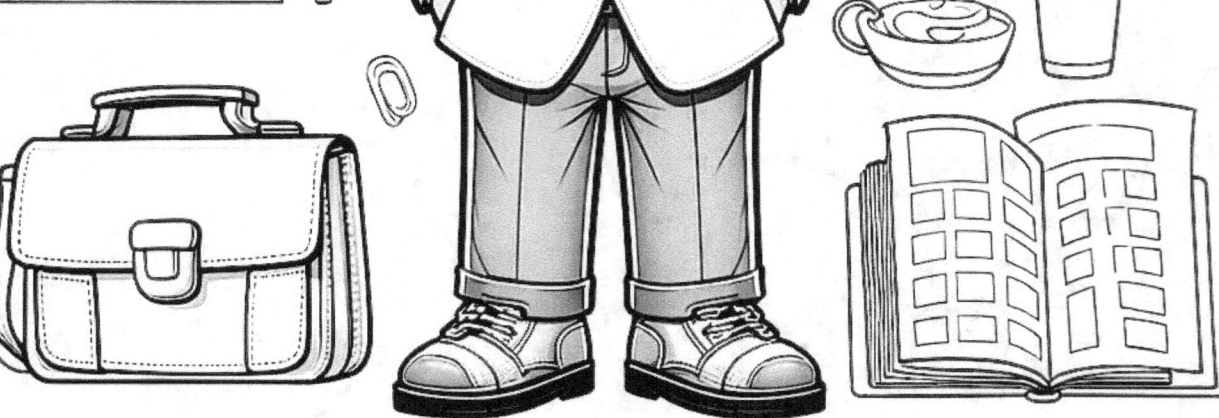

ENTREPENUER

F

Is for

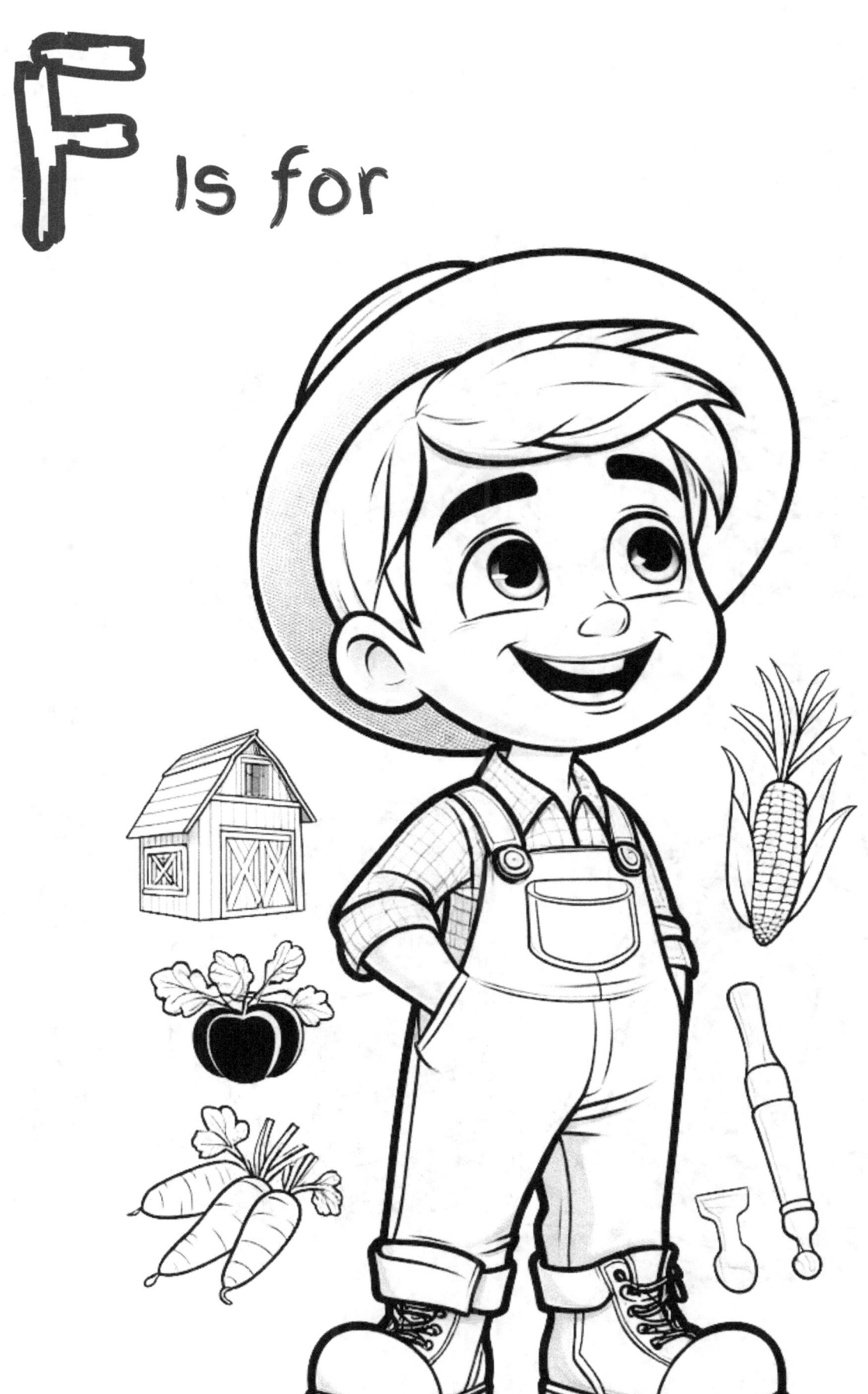

FARMER

G is for

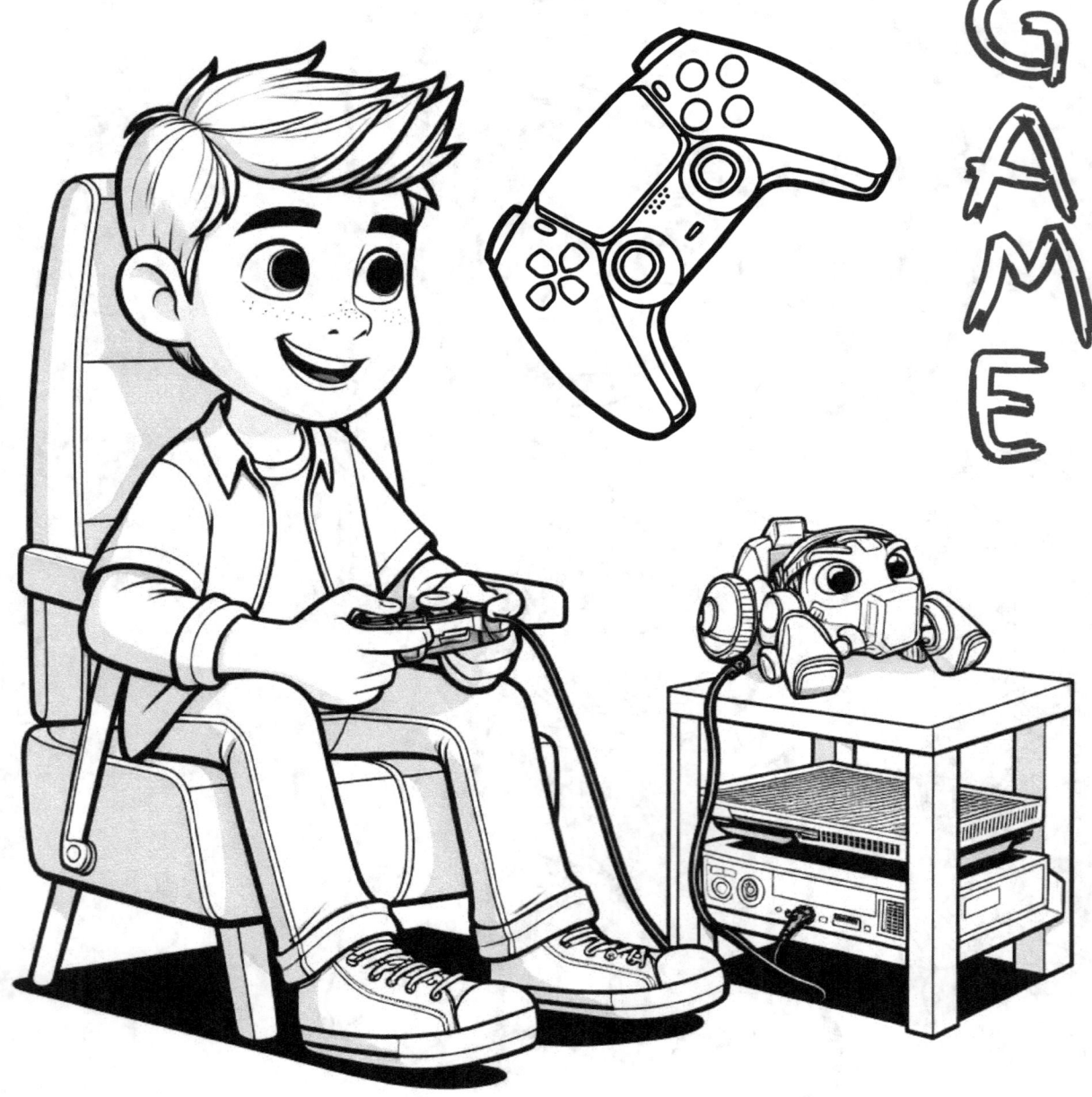

GAME DEVELOPER

H is for

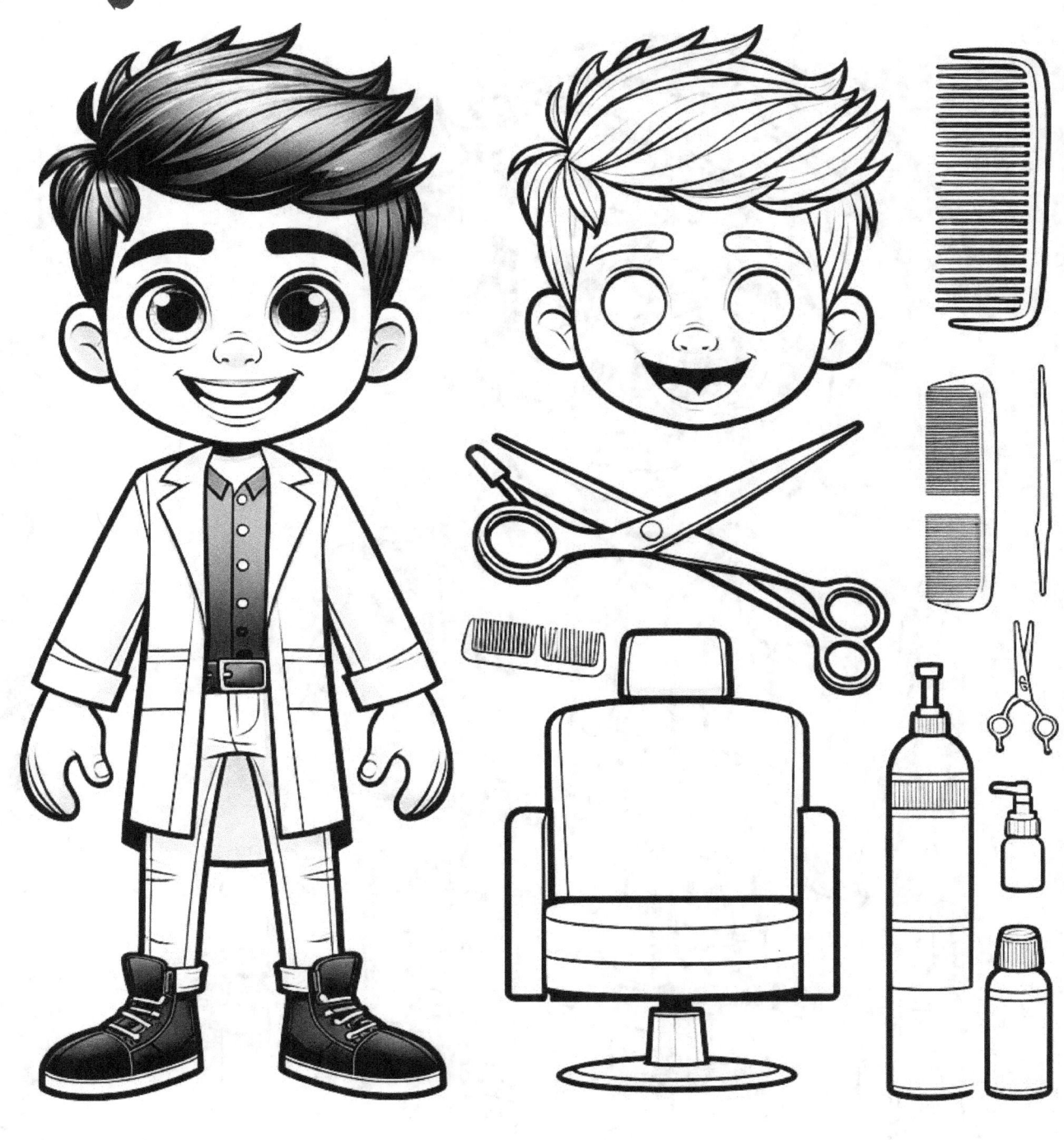

HAIR STYLIST

I Is for

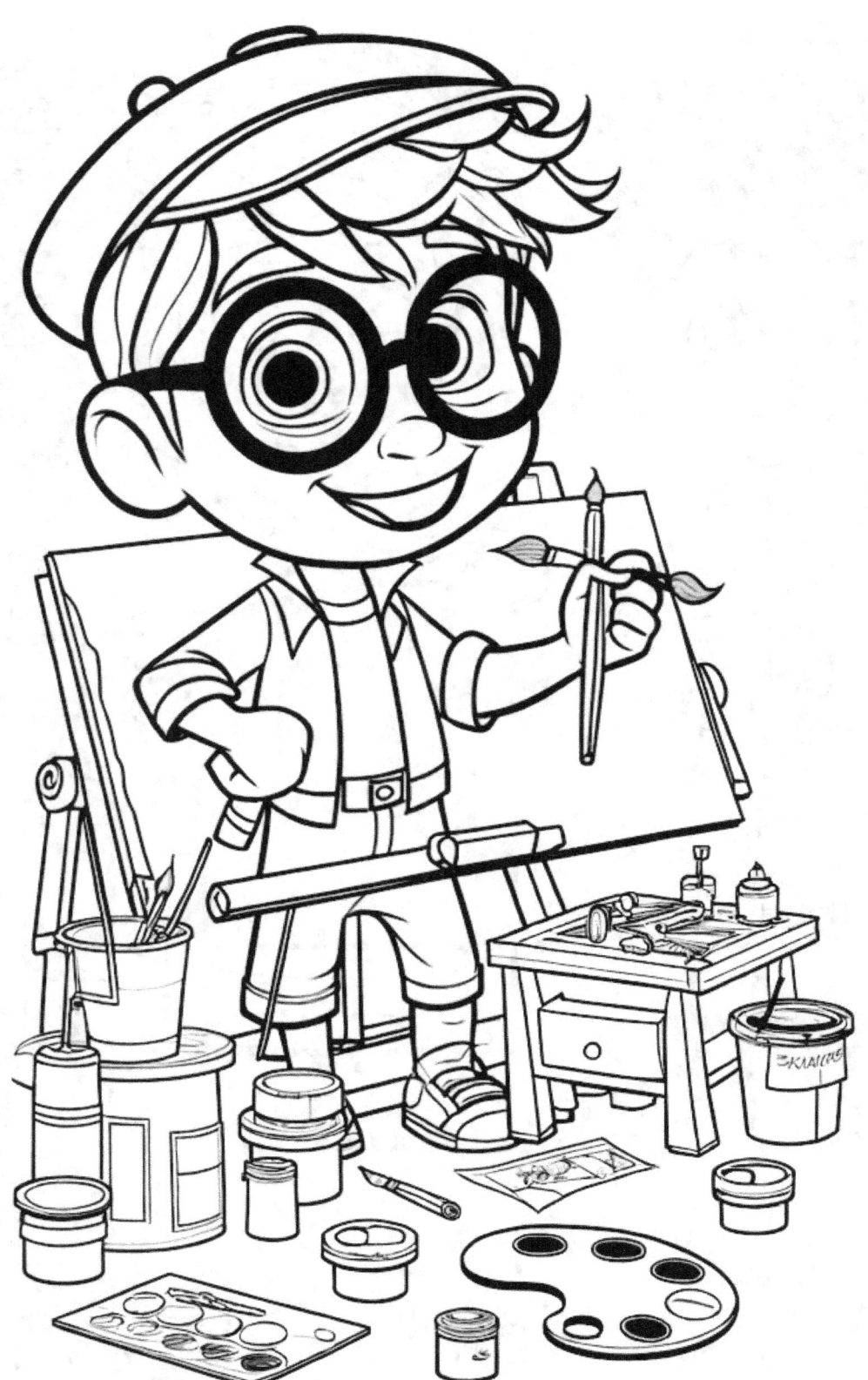

ILLUSTRATOR

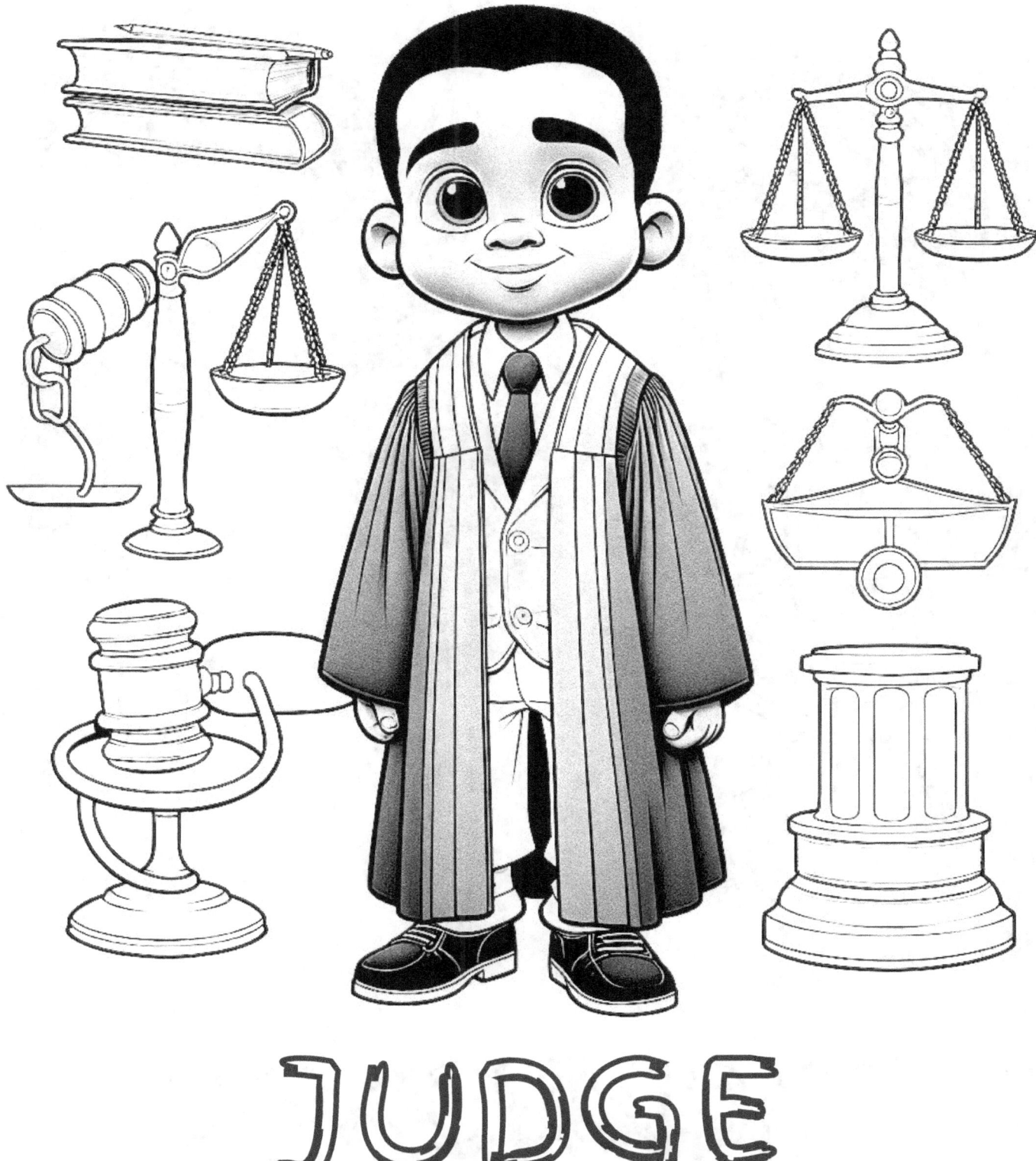

J is for

JUDGE

K Is for

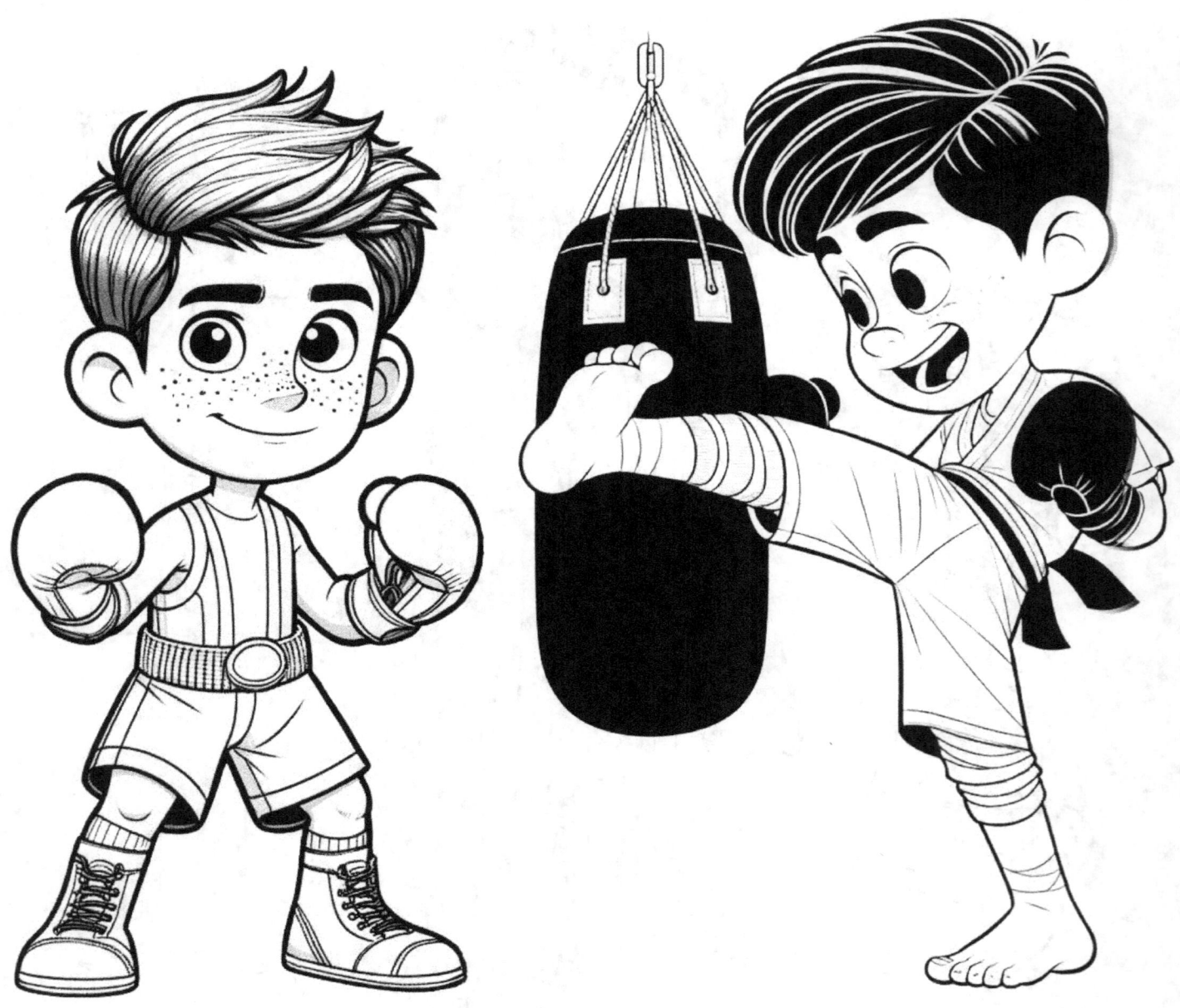

KICKBOXER

L is for

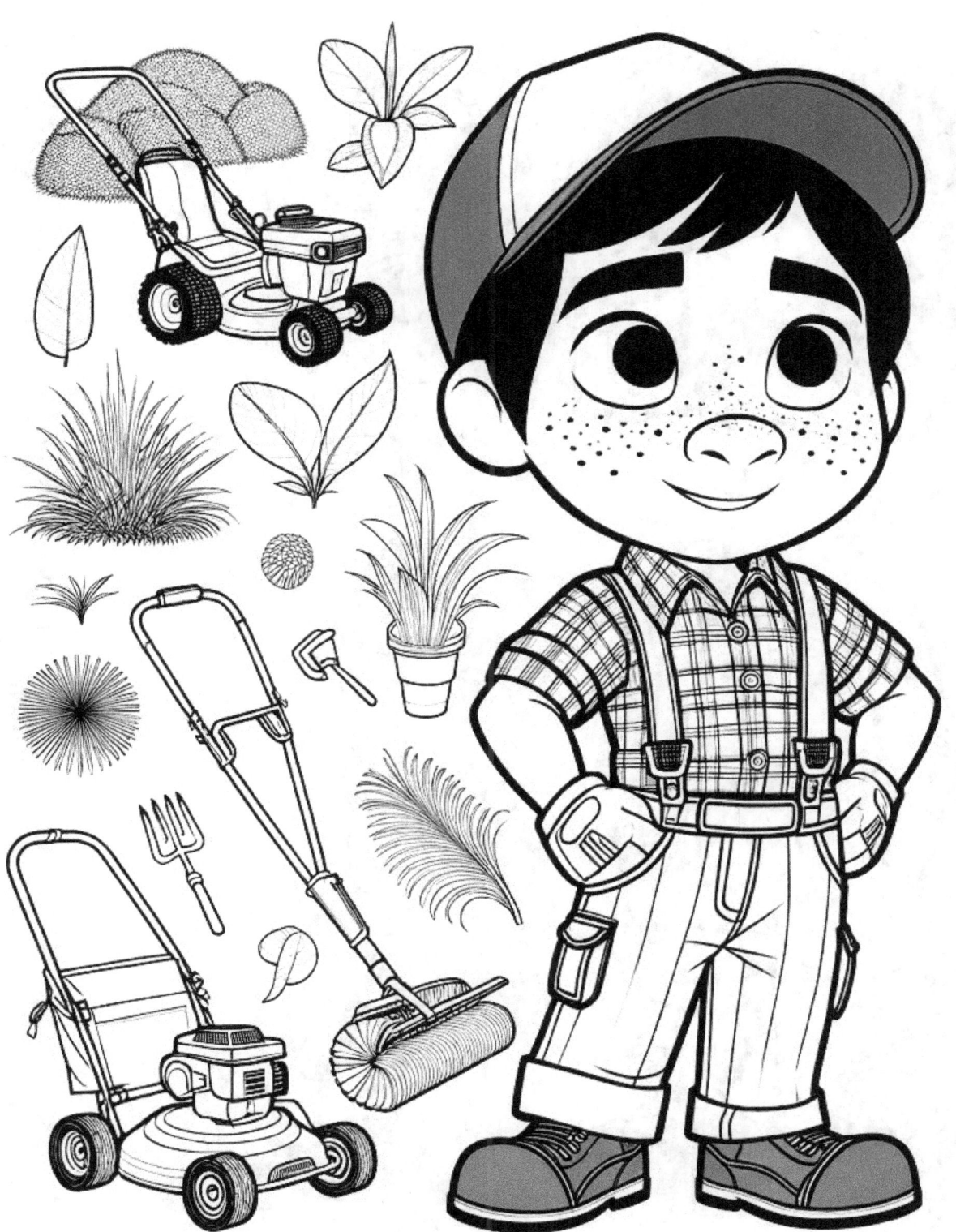

LANDSCAPER

M is for

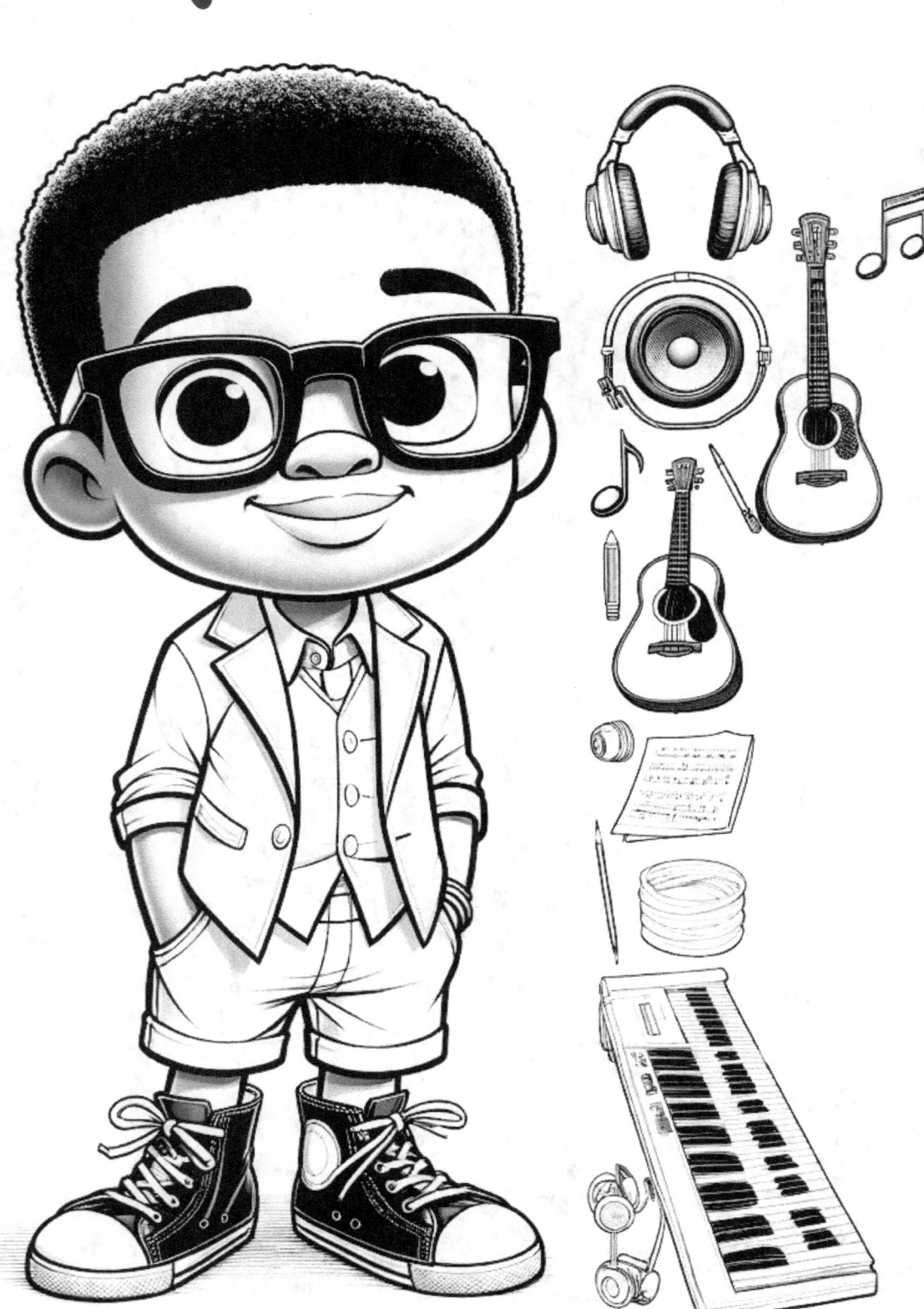

MUSICIAN

N is for

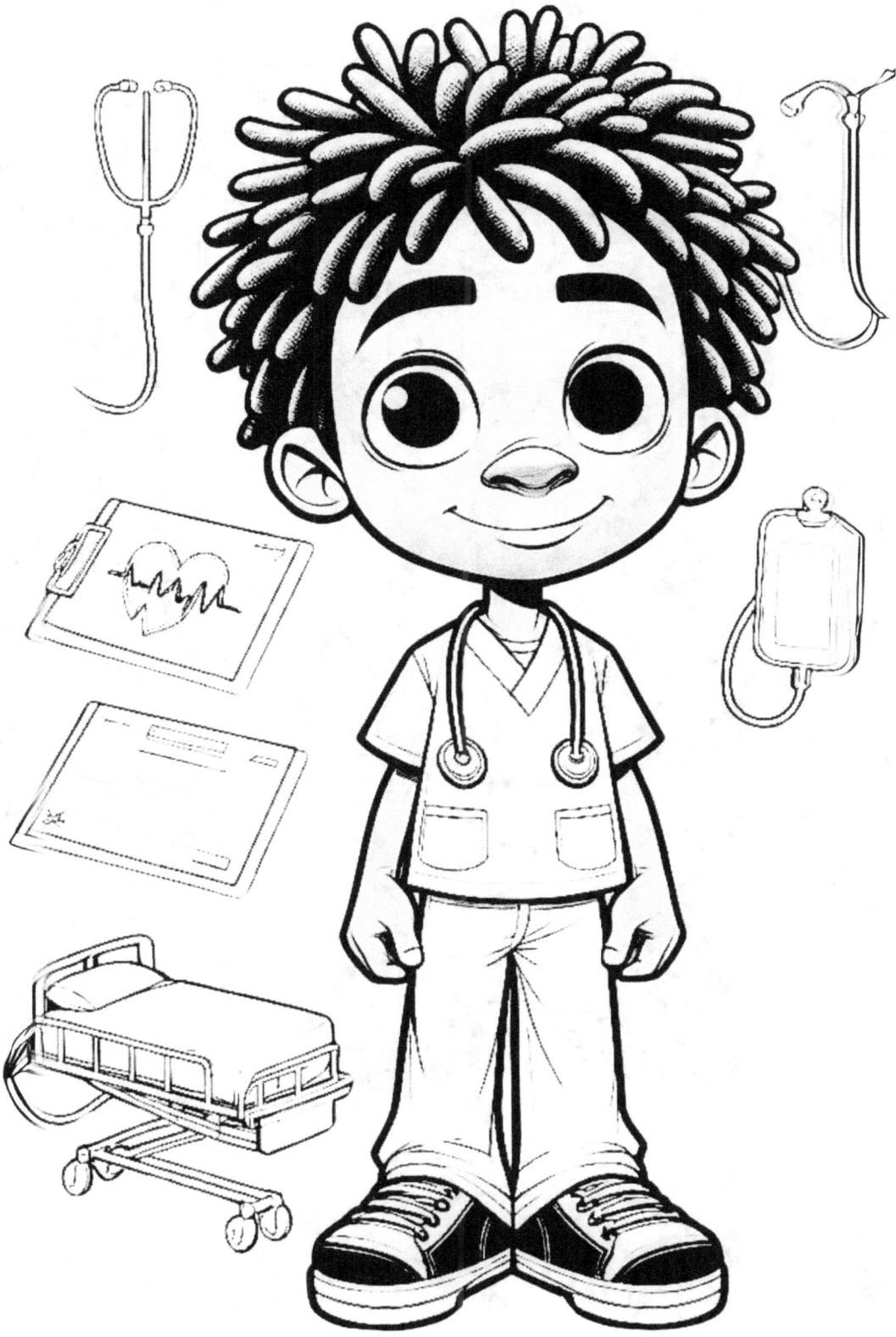

NURSE

O is for

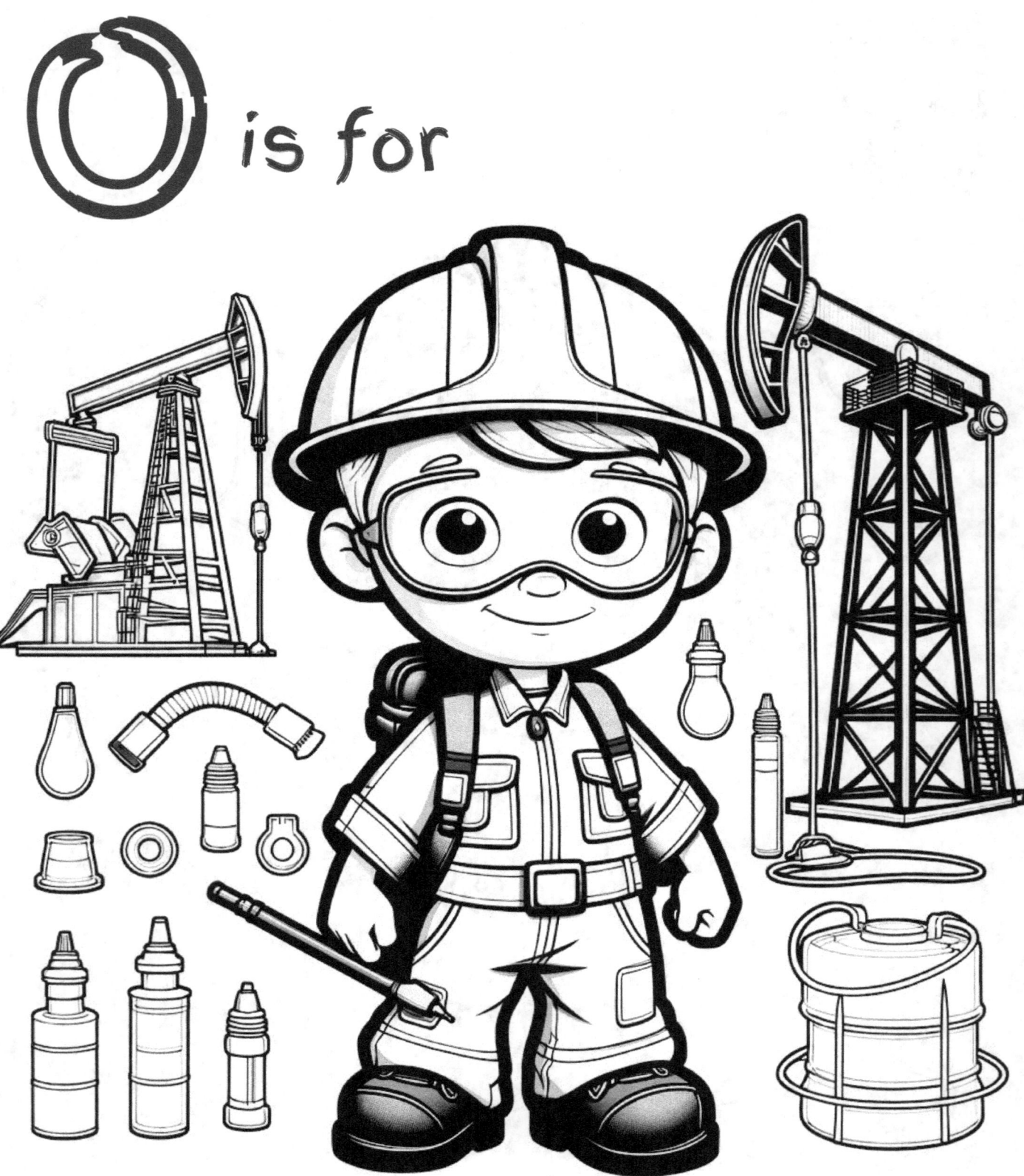

OIL AND GAS

P is for

PHOTOGRAPHER

Q is for

QUILTER

R is for

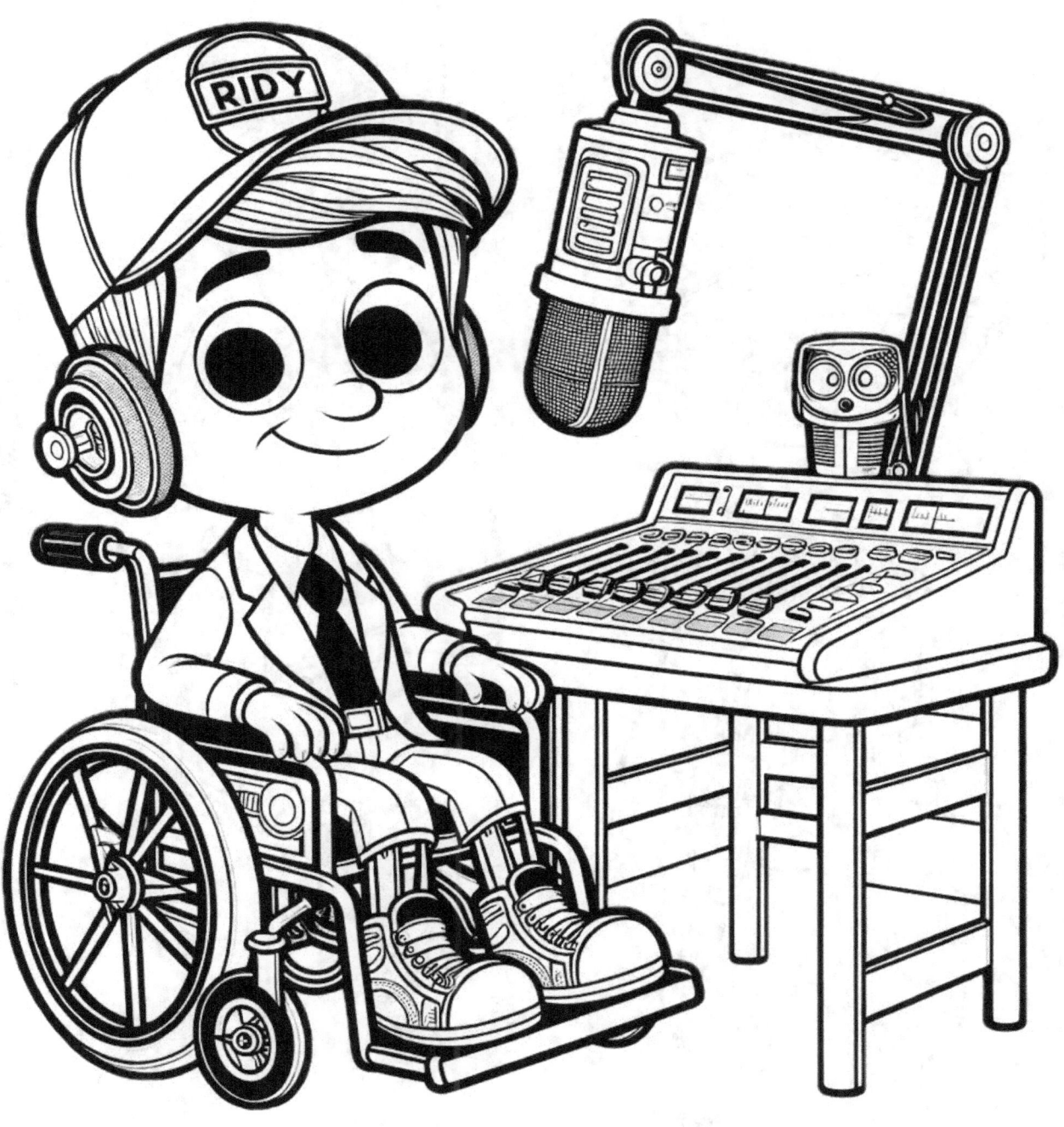

RADIO HOST

S is for

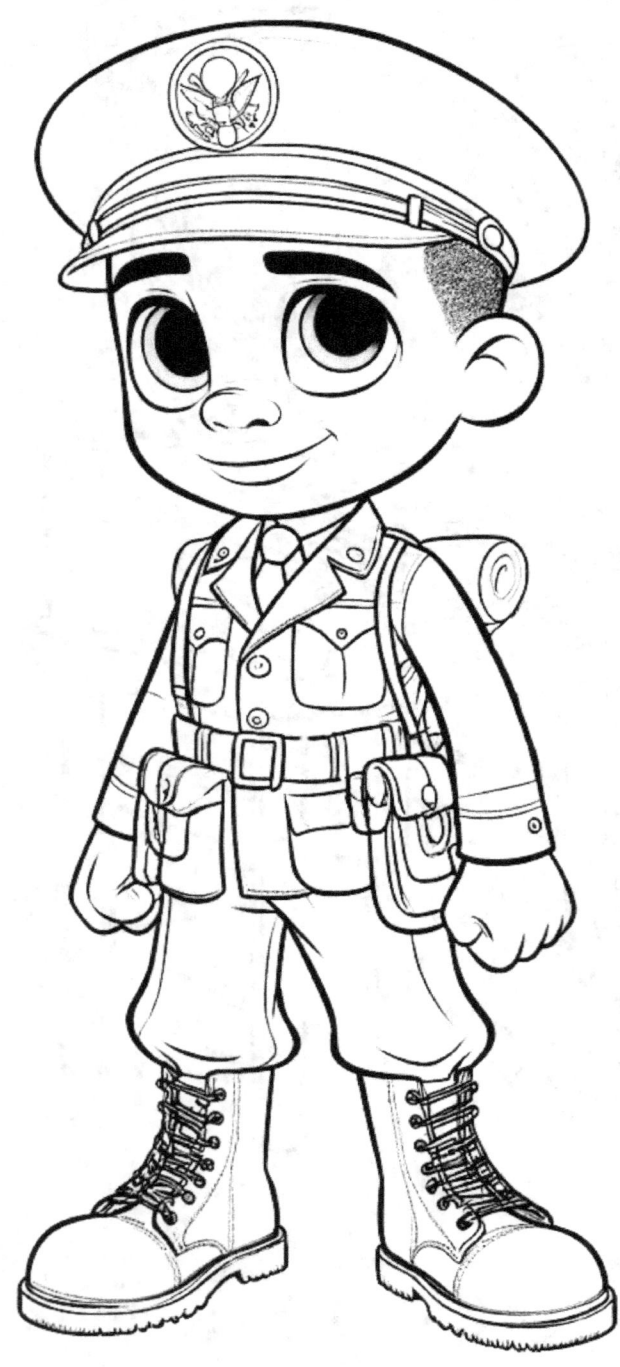 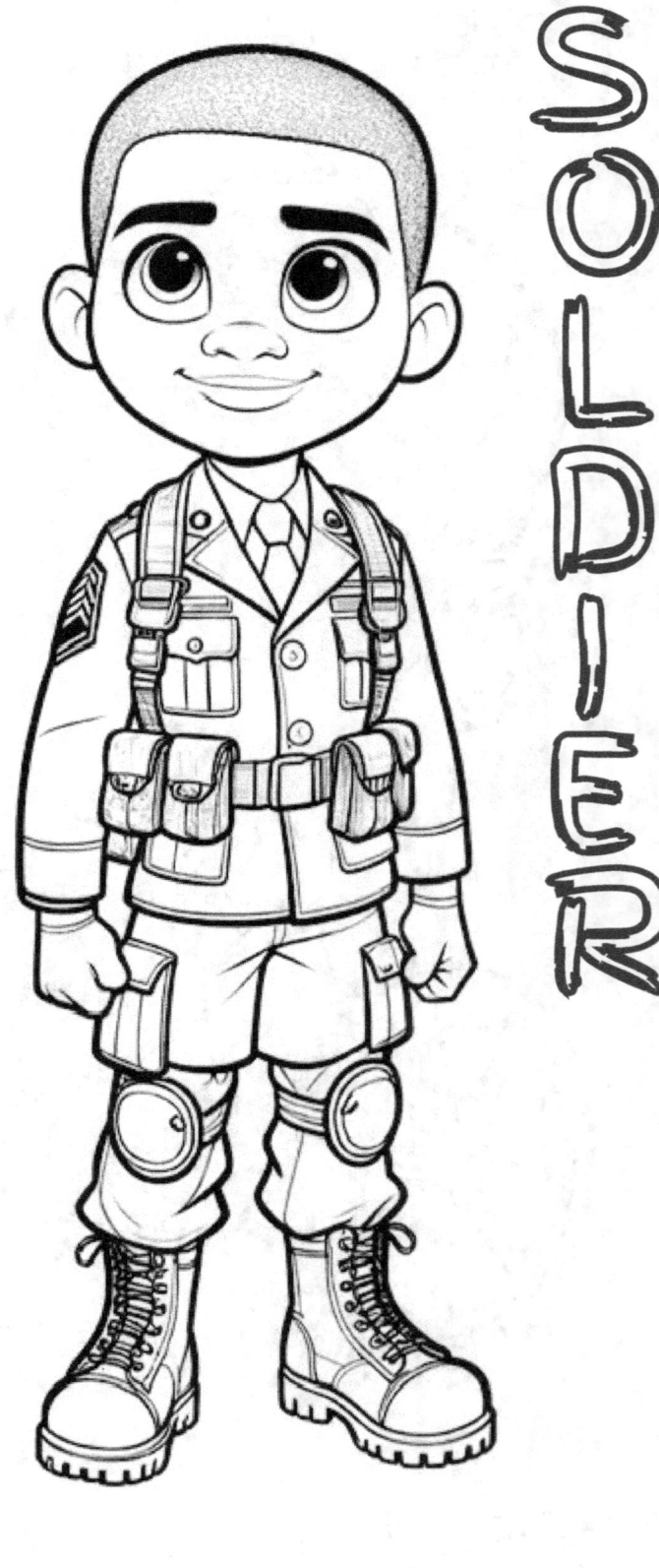

SOLDIER

T is for TEACHER

U is for

UMPIRE

V is for VETERINARIAN

W is for

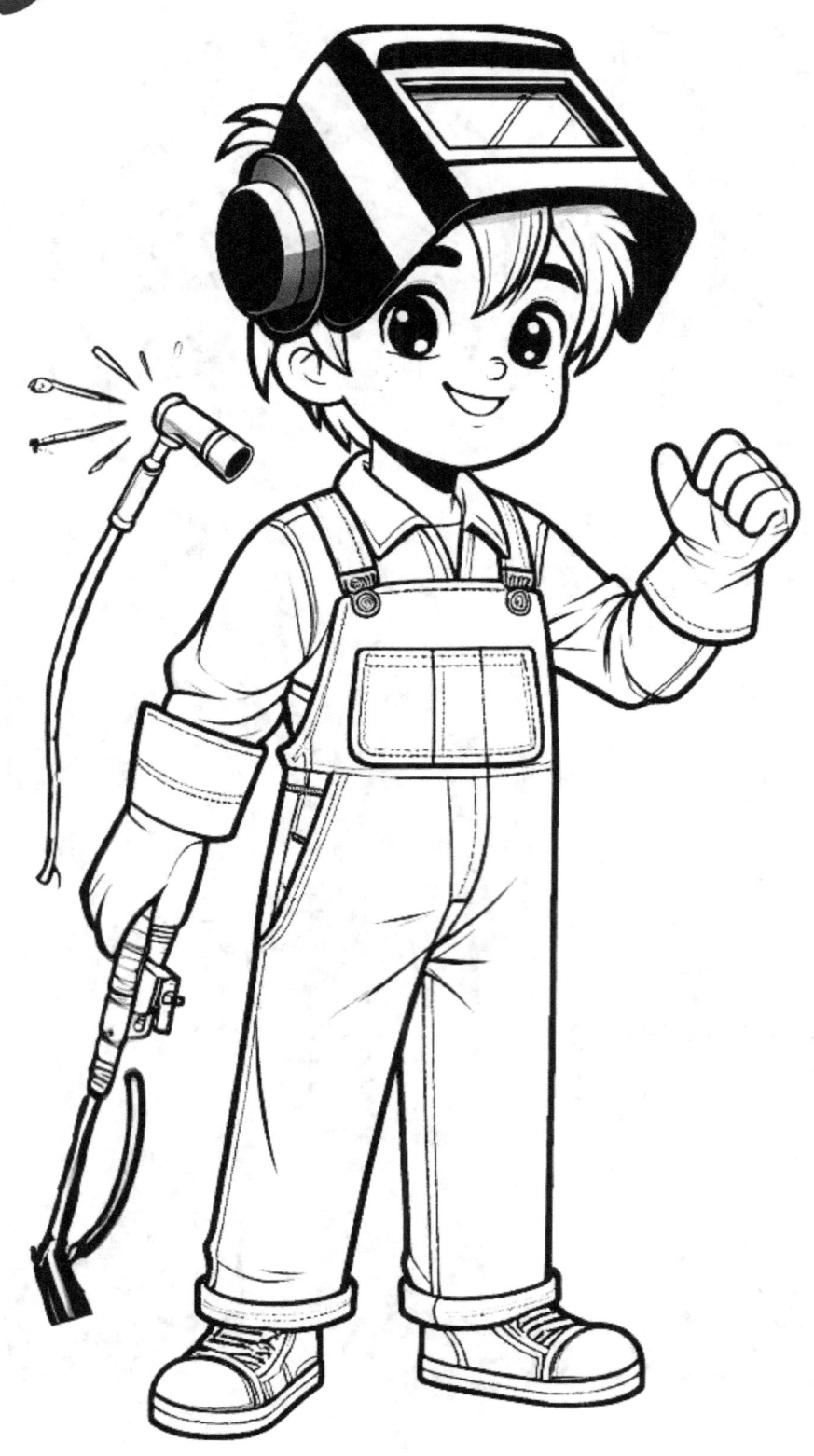

WELDER

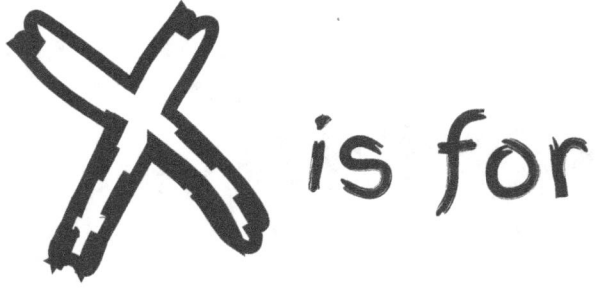 is for

XRAY TECH

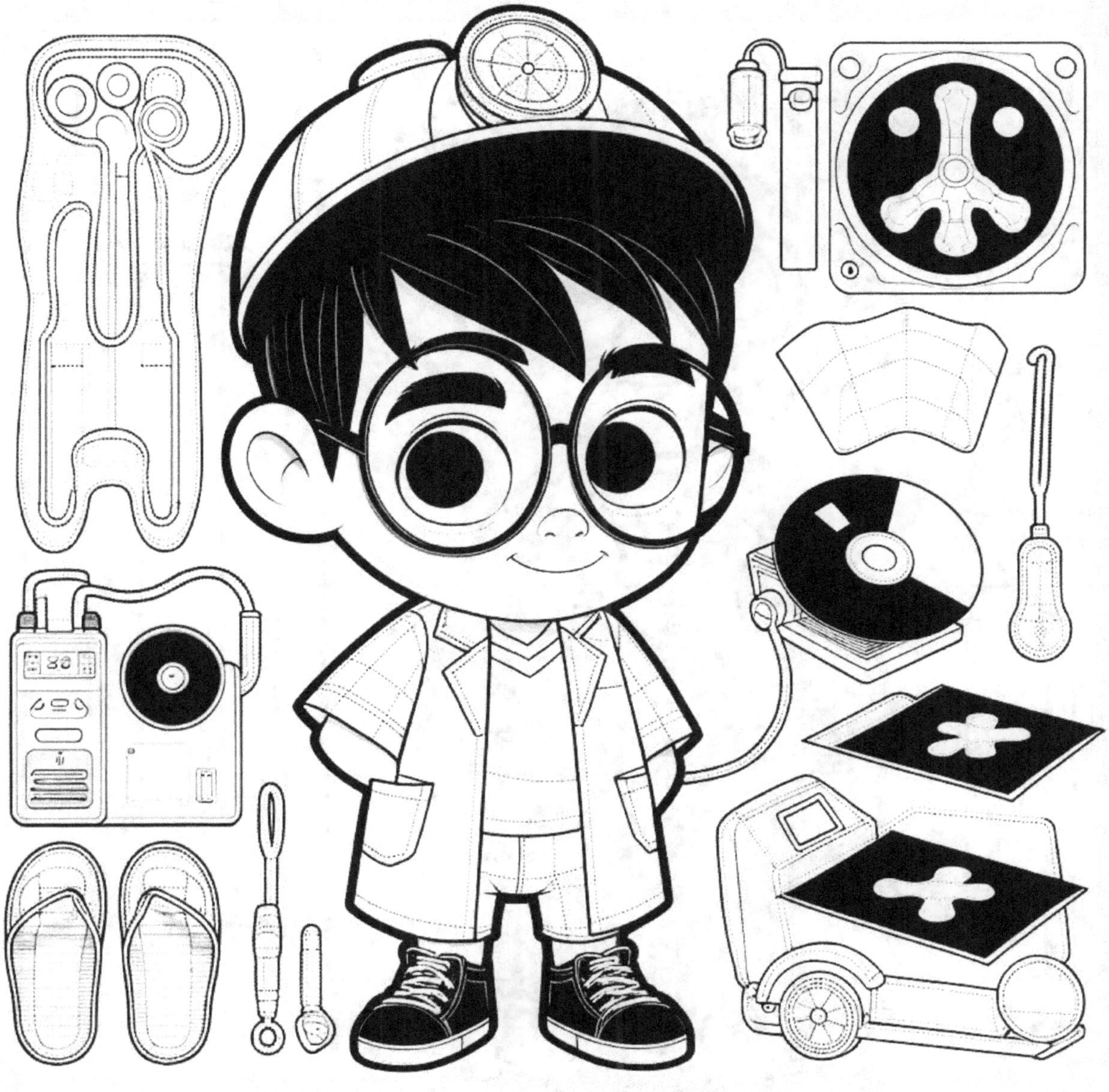

Y is for

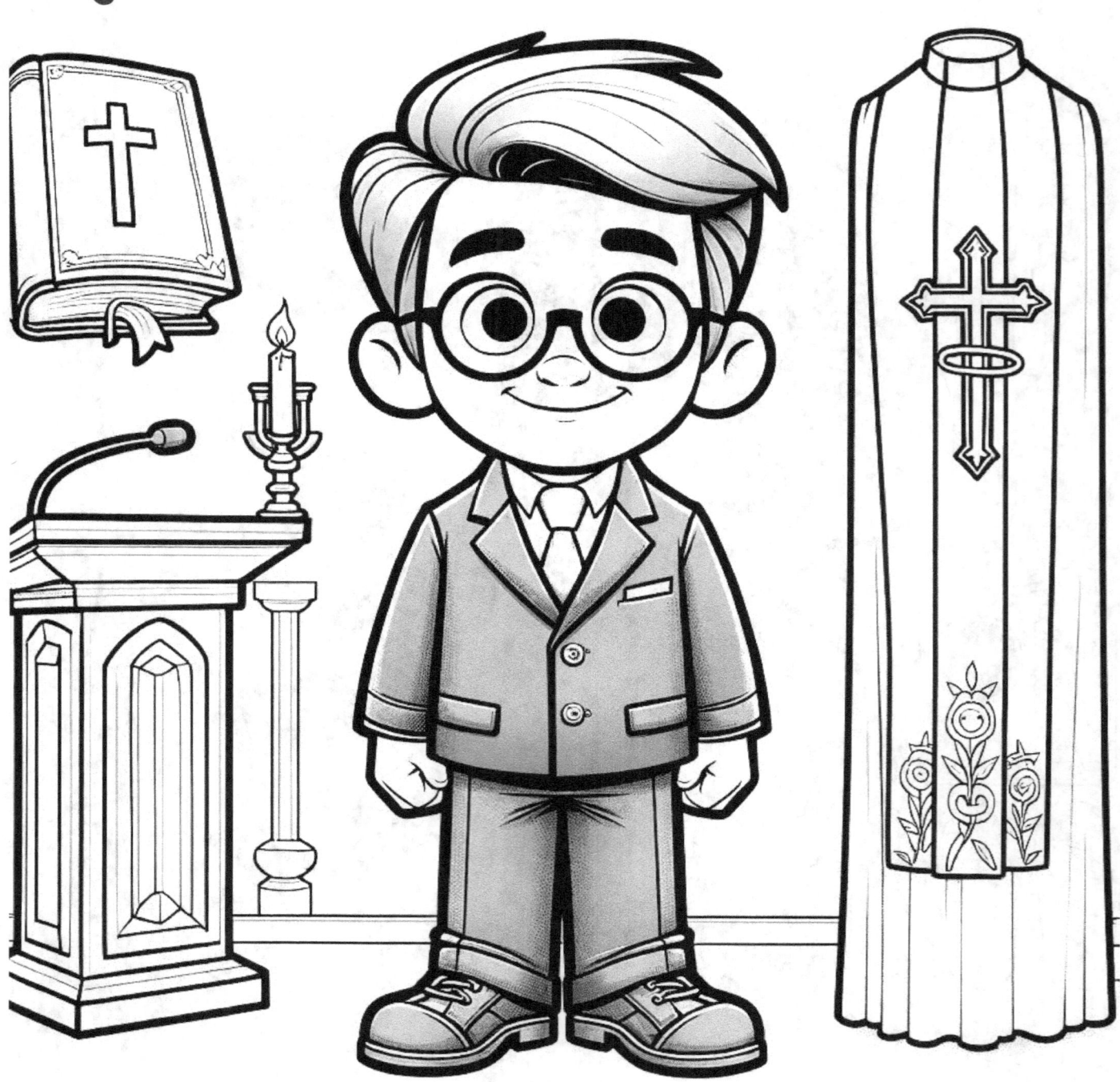

YOUTH PASTOR

Z is for

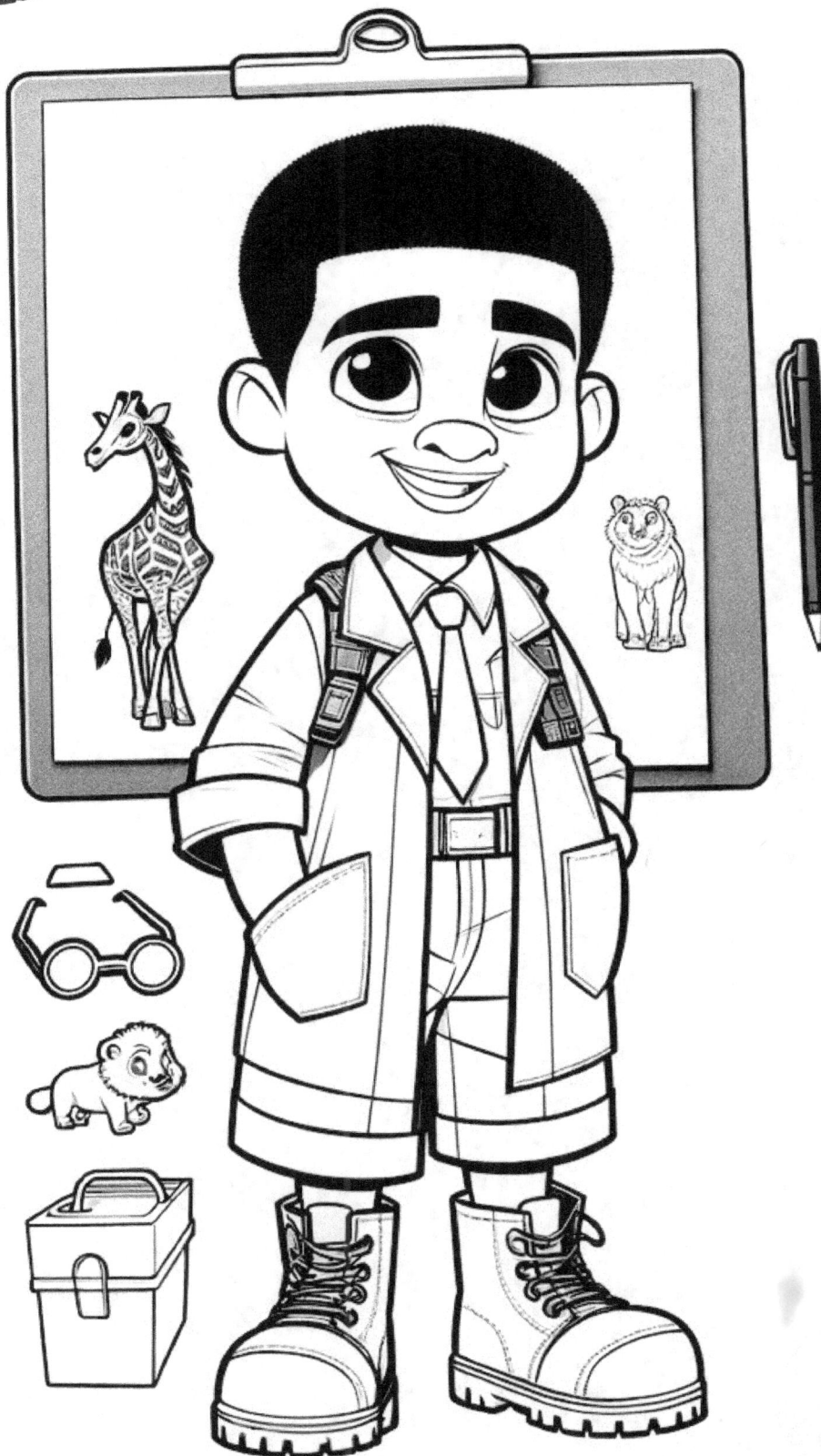

ZOOLOGIST